If You're Looking For Brightness

Finding Light: Poems, reflections and insights

Lauren Lott

Copyright © 2024 Lauren Lott
All rights reserved.
No part of this book may be used, reproduced or resold
in any form without written permission from the author.
ISBN: 978-0-6489466-8-7

For Lotty - I fell in love with the light in you.

CONTENTS

The Light In Love

The Escape Plan | 12
Keys | 13
Love | 14
Why I Opened My Heart Again | 15
To Love When Fear is a Viable Option | 16
Simple Acts | 17
How to Create More Love in the World | 18
Love's Ledger | 19
The Light in Asking | 20
Words to Read Aloud | 21
Discovering New Combinations | 22
Eternity | 23
Neon Flashing Sign | 24
Light Language | 25
In the Act of Journaling | 26
Why We Split | 27
Lasting Love | 28
Lumbering Light | 29
The Hidden Hand | 30
Suppose Love Has a Better Idea | 32
Binding Ingredients | 33
'De- (a prefix meaning intensive) Light' | 34
Afterglow | 36

Falling into Brightness | 37
Love Knows No Side Roads | 38
Love's New Shore | 39
To Love and to Warn | 40
I Don't Change the Vase Water | 41

The Light In Pain

What an Enlightenment | 44
Apology is Overrated | 45
Light Bulb Moment | 46
Forgive and Unlearn | 47
Far from over | 48
At the End of My Hope | 49
Hold | 50
Something | 51
Echoes of Betrayal | 52
Eclipsed Affections | 53
Bright Shiny Superfluous Claims | 54
You Can't Handle the... | 55
I Deserve Better and We Need to Learn | 56
Truth and No Trace of You | 57
Reasons Alone | 58
Artificial | 59
The Great Allowing | 60
Eternal Dawn | 61
This is How I'm Learning to be Brave | 62

Overboard | 63
Gathering Glimmers | 64
Courage and a Couple of Beers | 65
Hope | 66
Fear | 67
The Healing Facts | 68
Things Left Behind | 69
Why it Got Dark All of a Sudden | 70
Being Here is Progress | 71
The Weight of Silence | 72
The Body is a Beacon | 73

The Light in Living Things

Keep Courage | 76
Starlit Vigil | 77
Notice What You Notice | 78
Just the Three of Us | 79
As Quick as That | 80
Small Joys | 81
Despite | 82
Regardless of Shoes | 83
Light Therapy | 84
Recipe for Rapture | 85
Silent Bright | 86
In Trust That There is More | 87
Revival in Verdant Hues | 88

There is Always Something in the Stillness | 89
Signs That It Will Be Okay | 90
What to Do With Wonder | 91
It's Only Natural | 92
Between Blight and Bloom | 93
In the Light of Now | 94
How to Be Happy (It's Scientific) | 95
Cultivating Clarity | 96
On Your Side | 97
What to Do When You Are Unwelcome | 98
Wasn't It Good? | 99
Don't Start with the News | 100
Spectrum of Sight | 101
Catching the Sun | 102
Hindsight | 103
Let | 104
The Way We Turn | 105

The Light In You

In Courage | 108
A Decision, Then a Downpour | 109
And Then There Is That | 110
How to Turn the Lights On | 111
Gold Dust | 112
Thy Sparkle, Thy Shine | 113
Wonder Still, Wild Heart | 114

Held by Time and Connective Tissue | 115
Deeper Than Dapper | 116
Why There Is No One Like You | 117
Made to Transform | 118
The Radiance of Release | 119
Guidance Granted | 120
Common Kindness | 121
Breaths | 122
The Swap | 123
A Certain Ache | 124
Echoes of the Infinite | 125
Inner Oasis | 126
Isolations Invitation | 127
So Freaking Inspirational | 128
Joe Glow | 129
Feedback | 130
Little Fires | 131
Depending on Who is Holding the Mic | 132
Sigh and Release | 134
If You're Looking For Brightness | 135

The Light In Love

The Escape Plan

I set an alarm,

10am daily.

And when it sounds,

I say the words,

"May you be safe.

May you have peace.

May you be well."

Goodwill is my get-out-of-jail card.

To bless is to break free.

Keys

Love
is exactly where
you left it.

It is not lost.

Trace your steps.
Recall the last time you beheld it.
Check all the pockets of your past.
If you need to, ask a friend
to help you look.

Did you leave it in the lock
of someone's heart?

Did it slip down the back of your
comfortable doubts?

Did you accidentally drop it
somewhere along the path?

Love,
is exactly where
you left it.

It is not lost.

Love

Trust the slow work of it.

The patient, forebearing flow of it.

The impassive, persistant pulse of it.

The steady, sure exhale of it.

Why I Opened My Heart Again

I've heard it said,

"To forgo love is to render all meaningless."

And I wondered,

can one live without meaning, truly?

Unpersuaded, my heart does not believe so.

And in seeking meaning, found love.

And in finding love, fostered new light.

To Love When Fear Is A Viable Option

To the ones
who drag the light in
when they enter.

Those who shine
through their pain
and refuse to pass it on.

In a world that can be
so harsh, you show us
the true meaning of rebellion.

Simple Acts

I pour boiling water into a cup
and let the leaves infuse.

Milk?
Sugar?

I set it down before her.

Anyone could do it.

It's not about tea.
It's not about the way her eyes
soften as she mouths, "Thank you."

To dignify.
To honour.
To give space.
To listen.
To esteem.

Anyone could do it.

How to Create More Light in the World

Focus on

all the ways

you are loved,

and have been

loved throughout

your years.

Love's Ledger

I imagine my anger is a coil of coins,
stacked, wrapped in brown paper.

I slide them to the far side of the table,
having lost count of what has now
become so costly.

I don't know if it helps,
imagining emotions as objects,
putting them in front of someone
more equipped to deal with them -

Love perhaps,

but for now,
things feel better.

The Light in Asking

Ask delightful questions.

Who is dear to me?
How can I help?
What brings me joy?

See now how these words
have no regard for opinion?

See how they are undistracted
by our shortfalls?

See how they are not concerned
with who is in and who is out?

See how they perch before you,
willing to return delightful answers?

Words to Read Aloud

This is the hope we hold;
the new will forever dawn.

And although better does not
rise with every new day,

the backflow of life proves with time
that generosity, kindness and forgiveness

are as forceful, if not more,
than even the darkest realms of fear,

and will with fixed intent
deliver unto us, manifold facets of love.

Discovering New Combinations

Younger, I knew
without question
honey held hands with toast.
Summer and ice cream always kept in time.
There was nothing that could be paired better
with salt than pepper.

Older, I'm discovering
new combinations. Unions I didn't initually
think would work together-
like surrender and strength,
like wander and purpose,
like gratitude and grief,
like boundaries and love.

Eternity

We know.
We all know.

If we get low enough,
If we let go enough,

we see love is the only way
to clean up this mess.

We know.
We all know.

We were all sent the memo.
It is written on our hearts

Neon Sign Flashing

When I am confused,
when I don't know what is true,
there is a beacon, a sign, a flag-
a way to know what is real.

Look for loyalty, love in lights.

Light Language

Though some say we cannot hear
what does not make a sound,
I am learning to listen to light.

"There are things eager to be yours."

"You are not the pain you feel."

"What happened does not diminish your worth."

"You have significant work to do."

"Take as long as you need to heal."

"You are worthy of love and connection"

"Have Peace"

In the Act of Journalling

A prompt:

>How can I be more free?

Prompted a prompt:

>How can I better use my freedom?

This sparked the thought:

>What do I hold that remains untapped?

that lit up an understanding:

>I can give a little more love, and

opened the way to a gesture. In giving

>I am made free.

Why We Split

They say love covers all,

flows into every crack,

repairs every heartbreak,

fills every gap.

But I think

sometimes love is the crack.

It is the break.

It is the gap

that separates some people,

to liberate and protect.

Lasting Love

When we say 'light,'
do we mean grace?

Do we mean all the things
that could have happened
that didn't?

And even when we've seen the worst of it,
maybe the ones we love left too soon.

Do we believe that grace would say,

"In a world full of souls, isn't it wonderful
how you witnessed each other?

Isn't it wild how you talked and laughed,
danced and played?

They were a gift that you both
do and didn't miss."

Lumbering Light

I know the way love feels
when they leave:

punishing,

hard to do anything.

On bended knees,
silence and distance
beg to be filled.

Oh you, reading this.

Oh you, who may be brokenhearted.

Let love be heavy for a while.

There is so much to learn here.

The Hidden Hand

I have a story,
actually, a few,
about how coincidence
didn't feel like coincidence.

There was the time
I heard about B U T T E R F L I E S
appearing after she lost
her little offshoot.
And then, at 2 a.m.,
as I sought water,
I saw one circling the room.

There was the dream of packages
wrapped in string and brown.
Three months pass, and T A - D A!
Random packages abound.

There was the carefullly placed page,
left open for M E to read,
that lead to the discovery
of just the words I needed.

. . .

Do you have stories?
Just one, or maybe a few,
of how coincidence
didn't feel like coincidence,

but L O V E,
pushing up closer to you.

Suppose Love Has a Better Idea

Maybe there is another reason.

One that isn't based on my lack of emergence,
or your lack of integrity.

A reason that isn't about lack at all,
but rather, expansion, growth,
going from glory to glory.

It is good, at times, to leave all reason,
all blame, all assumed knowledge,
and believe in ways that are not our own.

Perhaps there are thoughts that are higher.

Binding Ingredients

Recipes are a kind of affection.

Add this to this and mix with that.

Works everytime - certainty, a surge of
the sublime.

We vow as long as we both shall live,
because promises are words, boxed
and wrapped.

Infallibilities - security or traps, tightly strapped?

I do not know how many years we will be gifted
or the paths that will be made open to us,

but I am sure of the way a flame lights the stove,

and if we lean in close to it we will simmer
and be seasoned with warmth.

De- (a prefix meaning intensive) Light

i.

Love likes to catch us off guard.

ii.

At the age of thirty-something, I found myself
singing to a crowd under a mock-up trojan horse
on the edge of the Dardanelles Strait in Turkey.
Ever since that day, I keep asking myself,
"Did that really happen?"

iii.

I was once crowned
the "Queen of Love and Beauty."
It happened when an actor,
dressed as a knight,
picked me from an arena of contenders
one surreal Saturday at Medieval Times.

. . .

iv.

In my teens, I wrote to an organisation.
They put my note in their newsletter.
In those days, nobody needed permission.
When I received my copy,
I read it continuously, astonished.
My words on their paper.
My thoughts in other heads.

v.

Consider the sublime, moments when
reality feels like a dream, and tell
your tired heart to stay open to surprise.

Afterglow

In this ordinary miracle,
the common often
overshadows the celestial.

It is not significant to live in a house.

Or is it?

Consider a house claimed
after one has been given away.

What about finding love
following heartbreak,

or flourishing again once first blooms have
faded?

Though the world is rife with strife
and senseless struggle, there is the
possibility of renewal.

Perhaps re-blooming is more regular than we
realise.

Falling into Brightness

Just like my twelve-year-old body
folded into a woman,

and my twenty-three-year-old dreams
morphed into reality,

just like my thirty-seven-year-old beliefs
were shocked into something new - love folds,
morphs, and shocks us into more of itself.

It grows brighter and brighter, as we fall
deeper and deeper.

Some wait to be moved; others know giving
way to love before it is felt only creates more
of it.

Love knows No Side Roads

I made a wallpaper for my phone
to remind me why I am here.
Is that normal?
Does anyone else do that?

I've always needed anchoring,
someone or something
to pull me from shiny distractions,
to keep me from floating
to the moon.

I heard a man who has really lived say,
"There are no tangents."
In the same breath, he uttered,
"Some things are too profound
to be captured on Instagram."

I made another wallpaper for my phone
to remind me why I'm here.
I don't care if it's not normal.
It's a photograph of the moon.

Love's New Shore

It wasn't good.
It didn't work.
It never could.

Stop with the stories
that tell you otherwise.

See now,
Love has brought you to a new beach;
a new freedom.

And the suffering?

Simply, transportation;
a way to get you from there to here.

To Love and to Warn

I am torn.

I do not want to show my chicldren
what you did to my heart.

I want them to love you,
to know the light of you.

Yet I know in time,
they will run into your shadows.

And I can't pretend I didn't know
how you could swallow them whole.

So I speak of you less now; a silence
that is both a sorrow and a safeguard.

I Don't Change the Vase Water

As soon as I saw her I knew
they were from them.

   These were not supermarket flowers,
   drawn together with cheap cellophane,
   petals bruised, leaves limp.

These were a declaration.
Every bloom, fresh, velvety.
Every leaf poised like a palace guard.

   And on a card, the mention of love.
   I place them in a corner and let them
   be lovely for a while.

Day by day I watch them dwindle.
There is nothing we can do to
save what wants to die.

   Like botany.
   Like seasons.
   Like us.

The Light In Pain

What an Enlightenment

Problems.

Regrets.

Mistakes.

Sorrows.

Failures.

Apology is Over-rated

S o r r y.

A word I have desired and despised.

It is both inadequate and enough.

Whether it comes to me or not,
hurt does not hear it.

Healing does not need it.

Light Bulb Moment

You'll see it differently
in the morning.

Maybe not tomorrow,
or by this time next Monday,

but one morning, you'll rise early,
open the curtains, and let in first light,

rejoicing in the sweet revelation
of what you once could not see.

Forgive and Unlearn

Remember the good old days;
advice that is not always good.

   Sometimes it is better to
   remember the hard times.

   That is where the light winks.
   That is where the truth sings.

And in listening we find
the will to never return.

Far From Over

This,
whatever it is
isn't the last thing.

It isn't the only thing.

Beyond this moment
there will be another.

In this plight
there is some kind of shelter.

A poem?
A prayer?
A presence?

This,
whatever it is
isn't the last thing.

End of My Hope

I will not search anymore.

If light be,
it can find me.

I will not beg anymore.

If mercy be,
it can find me.

I will not call anymore.
To be silent is to say more.

I will not work for it anymore.

If love be,
it can find me.

Hold

When it is time
it will be time.

But for now,
pull the darkness up
and snuggle down into it.

Cocoon in stillness
without chasing thoughts.

You do not have to rush after light.

Let it break in.

Something

There is light inside
everything that happened to you.

Not to say it was good.
Not to say it was fair.

Just to say
there is something to see;
to take
        and transform
                        into treasure.

Echoes of Betrayal

It ended
and as a parting gift -
disbelief.

How do mountains of joy
melt into rivers of sorrow?

How do tender promises
harden into lies?

We think we see
and then we do.

And then we do.

And then we do.

And then we do.

Eclipsed Affections

It is hard to accept
that you would rather
sit in the light of her candle
than sit in the light of mine.

I see you doing everything
in your power
to push me away.

Is it the pain?

Is it that you have found
a softer light?

One that is closer to your own.
One that isn't so bright.

Bright Shiny Superfluous Claims

Where you find lies,
you find truth.

Where you find truth,
you find freedom.

Where you find freedom,
you find love.

When you find love,
you will be glad
you didn't settle for lies.

You Can't Handle the...

If I were to pray for you,
I'd ask that you would be given light.

I would call on angels
to drag you from snug shadows;
away from the comfort of lies.

I would ask for the delusion
you cuddle up with,
would in radiance, vaporise.

And like eating a nectarless peach,
you would be completely dissatisfied.

If I were to pray for you,
I'd ask that you would be given light.

I Deserve Better and We Need to Learn

Though I miss you
and want you to return,

there is light
in your leaving,

there is good
in your gone.

Truth and No Trace of You

I admit
when I learnt of what
you really think of me,
all the moments
we shared together
felt foolish.

I showed up.
You weren't really ever there.

Though you filled the whole room,
I was entertaining a shadow.

When I turned up the light,
you were gone.

Reasons Alone

I wrote a list
of all the reasons
being here alone
is better than
being there with you.

It is only five lines long.

I spend most mornings like this,
convincing myself that
I made the right decision;
basking under faint light
I hope will get
brighter with time.

Artificial

You were never who I thought you were.

That's not your fault.

I have a habit of hurling glitter,
celebrating anyone who stays for a while.

It starts with a speck,
until eventually, they're sparkling
from hair to heel.

I didn't know it at first,
but this has been the source
of all my suffering;

calling commoners king,

creating shine
when I should just let them be,
accepting how they show themselves to me.

The Great Allowing

How good it feels
to let go;
to release
what refuses to be mine.
To accept promises
as untruths,
and let them
leave my mind.

Eternal Dawn

Pain can't stop blessing.

Rain can't turn off sun.

Night can't hold back morning.

Death can't conquer love.

This Is How I'm Learning to Be Brave

Some things

    need to stay

        where they fell.

        Love unreturned.

    Trust unearned.

Questions that bring no change.

Overboard

It's not personal darling.

People will do anything
to save their sea vessel
from sinking.

Jonah wasn't the first man
to be cast into the sea
when waters became choppy.

Souls have been walking planks for centuries.

And you floating there
in an ocean of tears
will not be the last.

It's not that people are heartless.

They just care more about the boat.

Gathering Glimmers

She steps lightly
between shale and broken glass,

stopping briefly, from time to time
to pick up treasure;

a pretty stone,
a piece of painted tile,
a shard of mirror.

It is clear that she plans
to make something beautiful
from shattered dreams.

Courage and a Couple of Beers

Thank you for your truth;

a shared story with no showy bits.

Your unmasking is my remaking.

Your openness is my closure.

Hope

It doesn't have to be felt to be real.

Fear

It doesn't have to be real to be felt.

The Healing Facts

I know it seems impossible,
but we can hold in our hearts
peace and pain together.

We can feel the rain of sorrow
while wrapped in sheets of calm.

We can grace the depths of grief
linked with relief, arm in arm.

We can ache while arching backward
bathed in soothing sun.

We can sense the light in darkest night
and hope when death has come.

Things Left Behind

A pile of things sits on my front lawn;
a broken lamp,
golf clubs never used,
a printer gone to the gods.

This will be the story of everything I own.

Eventually,
every fork,
every book,
every piece of furniture will be hauled into a hole
in the ground.

We too,
will one day
be declaired useless,
and even the memory of us lost.

Pain likes to make us forget our imperminance;

to forget that eventually, every story will surrender
to the light.

Why It Got Dark All of a Sudden

"Watch," says Trust. "Do not fret.
Transistions are meant to feel like this."

Being Here Is Progress

Still wonder.

Still trust.

Still offer yourself up
to each new day.

Still lift your face to the sun.

And if these things
feel impossible;

pain too hot,
loss too heavy,

stll breathe,
knowing every exhale,
every inhale
is a step
towards the light.

The Weight of Silence

Nobody taught me
how to be quiet with pain,
to accept it, to caress it
like a capricious animal,
heavy in my lap.

After hours howling with it,
which was necessary,
which was perfectly admissable,
the season for silence surfaced.

Hush, be quiet, trust.
Hush, be still, don't rush -
the healing, delieverance if you will,
depends not on you.

Your only task now
is to rehearse relief,
which is to say,
hold your peace.

The Body Is a Beacon

Sometimes shoulders speak.

  Backs and bellies jabber on
  about this and that.

   The brain sends a message saying,
   'get out of there', and immediatly
   feet start running.

   Someone once told me they loved me.
   Though motionless I left the room.
   I'm sure they mistook my silence for unkindness.

Pain can supersede the nervous system in spaces
where we are unheard.

The Light In Living Things

Keep Courage

You are moving forward
though it may feel like you are not.

Do you not know
when one climbs a moutain
one must spiral up?

When circling seems to be
all you are doing.

And resistance feels like
things arn't improving,

faint not, dear heart.

Starlit Vigil

How do you feel when you
hear the word 'mircle'?

I can not lie.
I can not help but hope.

Though I have been
debilitatingly disappointed,
still, I am like a child,
watching the night,
searching for stars,
believing that soon,
one will fall into my lap.

Notice What You Notice

There are signs.
Flickers of light.
Indications of what
will come next.

Do not think
that you do not
see them.

Do not talk yourself
out of what you know.

Life is a series of patterns.
Take your finger
and connect the dots.

Soon you will see it appear,
and appear,
and appear,
and appear.

Just the Three of Us

Sometimes,
I sit facing the sun,
allowing warm light
to rest on my eyelids.

In my imagination
I set everything free.

There is no time to save,
no burdens to bare,
no duty to fulfil.

There is just me,
the sun and love.

As Quick As That

One word.

One stroke.

One small act.

One change of mind.

One memory recollected.

One gensture from a king.

And suddenly,

your down is up.

Your bottom is top.

Your out is in.

You're back to where you started.

Small Joys

Little wing.
Little petal.
Little leaf.
Little snail.

Little twig.
Little pebel.
Little stem.
Little trail.

Lead me to joy,
like wild things do.

Despite

You are going to flower.

Things do not have to be
anything other than what they are.

Though pain.
Though shortfall.
Though struggle.

Right here among thorns
and small creatures that bite.

You are going to flower.

Reguardless of Shoes

I scoot back
out of shadow
into a lick of sun.

Sometimes we have to
position ourselves;

to run out into wild grass,
hands cupped,
face up,
ready to catch what will come
from behind clouds.

Light Therapy

Stretched out on a broken banana chair,
basking beneath a ball of fire.

It's Thursday afternoon
and I'm sure I should be somewhere,
doing something.

Conquering the world maybe?

Instead, I am here conquering within.

With sunlight.

Recipe for Rapture

Unlike your comfortable dwelling
the wild has millions of doors.

Look under rocks.
Pull back reeds.
Push up and see things
from high branches.

Wonder is potent
where wild meets heart.

Silent Bright

Things are rarely talked out.

One story becomes two,
and when retold,
two becomes many.

Nobody wants to be the villian in the story,
so we tweak it,
create a new tale,
one that captures a scapegoat,
downplays our dealings,
and upscales excuses.

Soon,
the only thing that sits right is silence,
and we disappear
like frost come noontime.

In Trust That There is More

Why light a candle?

Why look up at towering pines -
wise in their reach?

Why journey in search of a rare stone
or a far-flung star?

To fix ourselves inside a larger frame?

To acknowledge the existence of
everlasting knowing?

To take the hand of glory and entangle our fingers?

To feel irrepressibly alive?

Revival in Verdant Hues

When everything seems ordinary;
   the new feels like the old,
      heed what is green.

Look for what is growing,
   for anything emerging from the earth,
      and remember what can come from a seed.

It's remarkable,
   marvelous even,
      though it happens everyday.

There is Always Something in the Stillness

This morning,
the call of a bird
reminded me
that the world
is full of worlds,
and we are
full of imaginings.

How many ideas
do you think
you have had so far
in your lifetime?

How many possibilities
dance before you
in one day?

Like fireflies,
they can only be caught
by embodying stillness.

See now
how layers of light
hover around your chest
ready to be
scooped up into
the bottle of your heart.

Signs It Will Be OK

I don't know how it works.

A weather woman would be able to explain.

But when I wake to fog and mist.

What follows is the brightest of days.

What To Do With Wonder

Awe
does not need
elucidation.

It is but
a small birth
of awareness;

to be experienced
not explained,

to be surrendered to
not tamed,

to be perceived
as grace and
germinated
        into
              joy.

It's Only Natural

Like a bird is to flight,
so the soul is to light.

Between Blight and Bloom

September again,

And as expected, the acacia is in full flaunt,
the wind is warm and breathy;
pushing and sucking, tossing and throwing,
the light lambardas where weeks ago it lurked.

Yet all Septembers are not the same.

This year, not only are you not here,
but neither is the possibility of your return.

Yes, the flowers again flaunt,
and the wind again warms,
and the light again dances,
yet we hold not what withered in winter.

That's what Septemeber is for-

to show us what survived,
what wanted to return,
what was ready to bloom instead.

In the Light of Now

We shall get there someday,

but while we are on our way,
lets be here.

Here, with our lessons.

Here, with our choices.

Here, with what seems
to have chosen us.

For to not be here,
is to miss 'there someday,'

for being here is the way.

How to be Happier (It's Scientific)

Spend time with trees.

Cultivating Clarity.

To grow a garden
first you must
go outside.
Choose a plot.
Prepare the soil.
Push seed into earth,
and water it when
rainclouds wander
elsewhere.
And so it is
with any new flourishing;
it begins with
leaving the room.

On Your Side

See how the new day
dares us to reclaim.

Hear dawn whisper,

*'There is still time for courage,
for healing, for reconciliation.'*

Before parents rise
to serve the early meal,
morning has already supplied
uncountable possibilities.

What to Do When You're Unwelcome

Breathe like it is therapy.

Resist banging on doors
or writing on windows.

Tell the clouds.

Tear up under a treeless slyline.

S   c   r   e   a   m

(because there is no way to force yourself in.)

Look for anything that reflects light.

Take it into your hand, no matter how small.

Warm yourself over new wild and beautiful ideas.

Wasn't It Good

I thought she was magic when she said she was going to celebrate all the beautiful things that came into her life, even if they don't stay. I've always had trouble delighting in what is lost, no matter how many times it once took my breath away. I guess glimmers are found in knowing nothing ever really stays, and to have held, what is now gone, is grace.

Don't Start With the News

First thing.
Read poetry.

Then look out the window
and search for it there too.

"How will I know if I see a poem?"
I hear you say.

There will be within,
and all at once,
both a lifting and a grounding.

Spectrum of Sight

Sometimes
light
rushes
in.
Sometimes
it
leisurely
leaks
through
lessons,
or
laughter.
Mostly
it
likes
to
linger
in
one
conscience
breath
after
another.

Catching the Sun

Sometimes there are
certain places
you can't unfold.
That is why
the ground split
and your world fell away.
That is why
the sky cracked
and the stars
made their way to earth.

Dear One,
you are not buying time
waiting for fate
to change her mind.
Hold out your hands
and catch what is coming
towards you.
All you need
is one small sun,
one luminous orb
to warm you open.

Hindsight

We are specialists, aren't we?

Skilled at looking back.

Like children with faces to the sky,

who ooh and ah at shiny things

that happened millions of light years ago,

unaware they're looking at ghosts,

echoes of what was,

we scope our inner interstellar

for distant objects,

believing that somehow,

by doing so,

we too will find shiny things.

Let

Let them in:

    Lovely things.

Let them stay:

    Loyal ones.

Let them grow:

    Living seeds.

Let them go:

    Loathes and wishes.

The Way We Turn

See the way the flower faces the sun,
   bathing in its benevolence.

See how her body bends toward beauty,
   and in doing so becomes beautiful herself.

Fill your eyes with golden visions,
   and your ears with the bells of dawn.

Watch for goodness.
   Call everyday miraculous.

This is how we open up
   after clouds have parted.

This is how we stitch together
   endings that shine, and in doing so
     become luminous ourselves.

The Light In You

In Courage

She takes off her hat.
I can see she is still hot.
"It's ok, you're safe here."

She takes off her wig,
allowing me to witness
more of her story.

It's an honour, isn't it,
to really see people,
to be handed their
vulnerabilities.

That's where the light beams.

A Decision, Than a Downpour

AirPods. EDM. PNAU pumps "She moves with the weather," and ironically it starts raining.

Powder lands on my lashes, making it hard to see. But I am unfazed because finally, relief. This is not my usual stroll. I am walking free.

I see the sign my heart holds up as I push myself uphill and homeward: "Finally, you are following me."

That's what happens after making h(e)ar(t)(e)d decisions - powder, a light sprinkle, a little cry, and the weight lifts like water wafting into air.

And Then There Is That

Light is in receiving.

See what love offers you now.

Is there something you have overlooked?
Someone you have taken for granted?
Somewhere safe you can stay
in this senseless world?

Who returned home last night?
There was a small possibility
they would not, you know?

Even when grown children
step in loudly after midnight,
in darkness, let your tired heart
light up like a city.

How to Turn the Lights On

Say thank you. Say thank you. Say thank you.
Say thank you. Say thank you. Say thank you.
Say thank you. Say thank you. Say thank you.
Say thank you. Say thank you. Say thank you.
Say thank you. Say thank you. Say thank you.
Say thank you. Say thank you. Say thank you.
Say thank you. Say thank you. Say thank you.
Say thank you. Say thank you. Say thank you.
Say thank you. Say thank you. Say thank you.
Say thank you. Say thank you. Say thank you.
Say thank you. Say thank you. Say thank you.
Say thank you. Say thank you. Say thank you.
Say thank you. Say thank you. Say thank you.
Say thank you. Say thank you. Say thank you.
Say thank you. Say thank you. Say thank you.
Say thank you. Say thank you. Say thank you.
Say thank you. Say thank you. Say thank you.
Say thank you. Say thank you. Say thank you.
Say thank you. Say thank you. Say thank you.

Gold Dust

We are not fragments of life;
meaningless beings adrift.
We are life in fragments;
the sun squeezing through little rifts.

Thy Sparkle, Thy Shine

Though the world can be unkind,
it is true that you live here in it.

Do not make little of the mircle
that is your life.

What will you give?

How will you help?

I hope your answer is love
and with heart.

Wonder Still, Wildheart

See her dark hair
wind dance in the night.

See her tread pebbles
under lantern light.

See how she heads
toward a lone boat.

See how she climbs in,
sits, and floats.

See the river drag
the vessel from the shore.

See her surrender,
using not rudder or orr.

See her look up at
a sky full of shimmer.

See her chest broaden
as stars burn within her.

Held by Time and Connective Tissuse

There is light
in our limitations,
which is to say,
hold your heroes lightly.

Deeper Than Dapper

Sometimes, I don't realise I'm unlit, in darkness, until someone steps in, ablaze. They are the lightning in my storm and for a mass of collected moments illuminate everything, gifting hope and clarity - even when I didn't know I needed it.

They may be simple, seemingly unsuccessful, not appealing to the eye, supremely ordinary on the outside, but their words, their ways, their kind smile, oh what a light!

Why There Is Nobody Like You

1. The unquie rhythmic contraction and relaxation of the heart mussel.

2. The patterens made by the ridges and grooves on the tips of fingers.

3. The coloured part of the eye.

4. The lines on the soft, movable structures forming the opening of the mouth.

5. The frequencey of the sound produced by using the lungs and vocal folds in the larynx.

6. The combination and expression of traits.

7. The narrative that groups a specific number of days, threading together time and memory.

Made to Transform

It's ok to change.
It's not like you can help it.

How do you unknow what has been
made known to you?

How do you unfeel, unsee, unexperience?

Trying to do so would be to
miss the point of being here,
in this place to which you have come.

So when they say,
"You've changed,"
know it is nothing but growth,
and answer them by saying,

"Yes, and I will change again."

The Radiance of Release

I read today that a star shines brightest just before it bursts. Maybe, our most glorious moments are when we let go.

Guidance Granted

6:03am - Front verander. Sipping coffee. Organising ambiguity.

6:05am - A remembered conversation. An odd kind of inquisitiveness. A spark.

6:06am - Googling. Reading about the reason things fell apart.

Common Kindness

Unexpected light.

You know the kind:
a smile from a staranger,
help from a neighbour,
forgiveness when you've
been hanging with blame
for so long.

There are days that turn
on the simplicity of
s e l f l e s s n e s s.

We can burn.

We can be bright like this.

Breaths

26.

26 thousand.

26 thousand gifts.

26 thousand gifts a day.

The Swap

To live
larger,
braver,
fiercer,
that is what
I tell myself
I am still here for.

Why else is
year upon year
given, if not
for growth?

And isn't it
wonderful
how we get
to trade a
younger body
 for a
WILDER
soul.

A Certain Ache

I suppose
  looking up
starts with
  some kind
of longing,

  for hope,
for awe,
  for more.

Could it be
  soul seeking?
Searching?

  Could it be
spirit speaking?
  Birthing?

Echoes of the Infinite

What a thought.
What a rumination.
That we may be
the universe exploding.

The edge and not
the centre.

The ripple of startdust.
The result of Spirit's word.

Come now,
pay attention to
the brilliance
that is your life.

Think and be awed.

Inner Oasis

I've heard it said
that deep within us,
beyond every breakage,
every bad experience,
is a well, brimming
with light.

It cannot be
spent or spoiled.
It is safeguarded;
encirecled by love.

Tell me, what is more
impenetrable than that?

Isolations Invitation

To those who are afraid of being alone,
uninvited, not included, separated, unexcepted.

The day saves a seat for you
and so does the night.

See how they beckon what is in you to unfold.

Lonely is the seed breaking open,

is the pillgram pushing onward,

is the grave turning what was
into what will soon be.

So Freaking Inspirational

You have always been a mirror to me.

Thank you for every piece of exciting news,
every prestigious award,
every highly antisipated release.

Jealousy is a lighthouse,

guiding towards what could also be possible
for me.

I can live my own kind of dream;
every one of your Instagram posts proclaims
it.

Joe Glow

Occasionally,
I meet someone who
raditates a certain brilliance.

I'm not talking about talant or IQ.

They have a kind of hunger
for helping others.

Someone so egoless, it's magnetic.

They've learnt lessons,
survived storms,
processed pain to the
point of beauty.

But the best thing about them
is they show (in their own unpretentious way)
that it is possible for all of us
to shine a little brighter.

Feedback

Delete.

> Every third Thursday
> my imposter syndrom flares up.
>
> I want to erase myself from the internet
> and pretend I am invisable.

Restore.

> In courage, a woman sincerly
> thanked me for my honesty.
>
> She said my words made her feel seen.
> Her words did the same for me.

Little Fires

In winter, we gather
around a glow and spend time
with star-soaked skies.

For we have learnt
that all we need
to do to warm ourselves
and illuminate where we are
is strike a match.

And by that, we mean:
entertain alternative narratives.

Depending on Who Is Holding the Mic

I'm sure some still live with
the tweleve-year old versions of us.

Others are only acquainted with
who lives in the aftermath.

Several may cling to one thing
they think we said at one time.

Few are glad we are gone from their lives.

Maybe one wants to reconnect
but wonders if reaching out
would be appreciated.

There are those we see
from time to time
driving home or clutching a basket
in the grocery store line.

They say 'hello'
but what they really think
about who we are and how we look
we will never know.

. . .

There is the one who had a crush
but never told.

The ex-lover who we think moved on
but may still wonder if it could work.

And the girl we went to school with
who always sat alone, still remembers
our kindness or cruelty depending on who
we were at the time.

We are stories aren't we.
Stories told by different voices.

We are opportunities missed
or opportunities recognised; embraced.

We are gold found and washed of earth
or left in the ground; untaken.

We are light set free, uncovered
or hidden, snuffed, extinguished,
smothered.

Sigh of Release

Just like your body
s t r e t c h e s
out after a good sleep,
let your spirit,
rested and ready,
e x p a n d.

How good it feels to
u n f u r l;
to find the light
in small b e l i e f s.

If You're Looking For Brightness

Begin within.

Where soulful encouragement
meets creative expression

www.lauren-lott.com